Sip, Swirl, Savor

To Monica,
Savor Every
memory!
Beth
Gossip

ISBN: 1-4392-0741-0
ISBN-13: 9781439207413

Visit www.booksurge.com to order additional copies.

Sip, Swirl, Savor

A Wine-Tasting Guide and Journal

*Written and compiled by
Sassy Sommelier
aka Lizbeth Congiusti*

This Book Belongs To:

_____

Introduction

Ours is a big Italian family; my grandmother and grandfather came to America in the early 1900s.

My grandfather Bruno made wine in the basement. Most Sundays we would all gather together around the table and spend hours eating homemade pasta and drinking homemade wine. At some point during the meal, my grandfather made his way down to the cellar. The children would follow him down to the cellar knowing full well he'd be sure to give us a sample from the old, warped wooden barrel.

I know now the wine my grandfather made was not very good. The old barrels could no longer keep the air out of the wine, which made it old long before its time. The wine was dark like whiskey and smelled musty.

Yet every time I see or smell a wine like this, I don't think "bad wine". I think of days long gone, my family gathered around the table laughing and enjoying the moment.

While there are "good" wines and "bad wines", in truth a good wine is any wine that you enjoy. Use this book to help you understand why you enjoy a particular wine. Take notes so you will remember the moment and the people you shared each special glass or bottle of wine with.

The following pages are dedicated to my grandfather, Bruno, who made the wine and my brother, Joey, who taught me a lot about "good" wine.

Only by tasting wine do you come to know and understand which types and styles you like. The fun part is it can take bottles and years to become an expert.

But this book is not for those who want to become experts; it is instead for those who want to enjoy wine more. It is for those who wish to become comfortable drinking a glass of red wine when tradition dictates you should be drinking a glass of white wine. It's about knowing what you like and enjoying every sip. It doesn't matter what anyone else thinks.

I encourage you to take notes using the My Tasting Note pages to help you keep track of the wines you like and want to drink again.

I also believe it is just as important to keep track of the wines you did not like to be sure you don't spend your money on them again.

While drinking wine is the only way to determine if you truly like it, I encourage you to drink responsibly and never drink and drive.

Most importantly, enjoy every sip, swirl, and savor. Remember the time spent with family and friends and treasure the new experience each glass or bottle brings to you.

Best,
Sassy Sommelier *(aka Lizbeth Congiusti)*

Foreword

We other humans love complicated hobbies, and wine offers all too good a framework for satisfying that urge.

But! For those of us who just want to find something that tastes good with dinner, there is a forever thirst for a wine book that gives us just enough information to go along the store shelves and get along at dinner.

Enter Lizbeth Congiusti's Sip, Swirl, Savor A Wine-Tasting Guide and Journal, which gets rid of all the complications but does not sacrifice the nitty-gritty. Read. Think. Drink. Enjoy.

Bob Thompson – Wine Writer and Judge

Helpful Hints The Five S's

When tasting a wine, run a list of descriptive words through your mind. Then follow the steps below.

See: Look at the color: is it pale straw, Aztec yellow, blond, golden, green, gold, brick red, ruby red, deep purple, cranberry red, burgundy?

Swirl: Swirl the wine in the glass to release the aroma, bouquet, and fragrance.

Sniff: Sniff the wine in the glass. What scents do you detect: apple, apricot, peach, lemon, lime, pineapple, pear, baked apple, butter, butterscotch, yeast, asparagus, plum, raspberry, baked cherry, strawberry jam, prunes, mint, licorice, spiced tea, mushrooms, orange, chocolate, coffee, cigar box, pipe tobacco, cola, beans, almond, bread, biscuits, cinnamon, cloves, honey, ginger, yeast, gardenia, geranium, rose, honeysuckle, chalk, flint, grass, hay, minerals, stone, straw, gasoline, rubber, earth, leaves, grass ?

Sip: Swirl the wine in your mouth. How does it feel: full-bodied, medium-bodied, light-bodied?

Savor: Hold the wine in your mouth. Keep your mouth closed, then breathe in through your nose and swallow the wine. Take a moment to remember how the wine felt in your mouth: full, light, crisp, acidic, bitter, tannic, uneventful, or full and round, comfortable, savory, wonderful, or satisfying like velvet?

Words Used to Describe Wine

Aroma. General descriptive term for the smell of a wine. Examples include fruity, spicy, and earthy.

Astringent. A component in some wines that gives a drying sensation in the mouth, making your mouth pucker. Typical of young red wines with high tannins.

Balanced. Refers to the harmonious balance of the components of the wine (e.g., sweetness, acidity, tannins, alcohol, oak, etc.)

Body. The density or viscosity of a wine; thin, light, medium, or full-bodied. Can be seen by the way the wine clings to the glass when swirled (known as the "legs").

Bouquet. Not the same as aroma; bouquet is the result of the aromas marrying into a unified scent.

Complex. Describes a wine that is multidimensional in terms of flavor, aroma, taste, etc.

Crisp. A lively sensation on the palate, similar to tartness. Typical of wines high in acidity.

Finish. Term to describe the lasting taste of the wine after you swallow it.

Floral. The aroma of flowers found in Riesling and Gewürztraminer (jasmine, carnation, roses, violets, etc.)

Fruity. Characteristic of sweetness, richness, and body coming from ripe grapes or apple, apricot, raspberry, strawberry, blueberry, blackberry, lemon, lime, melon, grapefruit, peach, etc.

Oaky. The aroma and taste derived from oak-barrel aging, usually described as vanilla-like.

Spicy. Common spice aromas found in wine; include cinnamon, cloves, anise, and black pepper.

Wine Lingo

Professional wine tasters and writers have created a lengthy list of descriptive words to help us understand the characteristics, fragrances, and aromas of the many different wine varieties on the market today. Unfortunately, many of us do not smell the same scents in the glass that the pros do.

My suggestion is to find your own descriptive words to describe what you smell in your glass when you taste. If the wine in your glass smells like your grandmother's cedar chest, and that is something you like using to describe the wine, this will work well for you.

The same is true for the taste in the glass. Look for a taste you are familiar with, things you can identify and put a name to.

All the descriptive words are useless unless they can help you remember what is in your glass. Match the smell and taste of the wine to something you can identify and remember.

To help you build your vocabulary of descriptive words, take time when in the grocery store to smell fresh fruit, vegetables, flowers, and spices. In no time you'll have your own lengthy list of descriptive words.

Use the space on the next page to record your own wine lingo.

My Wine Lingo

My Notes

Wine/Grape _____ (write in or circle below.)

White: Albariño, Chardonnay, Chenin Blanc, Gewürztraminer, Gruner Veltliner, Marsanne, Muscat, Palomino, Pinot Gris/Grigio, Prosecco, Riesling, Sauvignon Blanc/Fume Blanc, Semillon, Trebbiano, Verdicchio, Viognier

Red: Cabernet Franc, Cabernet Sauvignon, Gamay, Grenache, Malbec, Merlot, Mourvèdre, Nebbiolo, Petite Verdot, Pinot Noir, Pinotage, Sangiovese, Syrah/Petite Sirah/Shiraz, Tempranillo, Zinfandel

Color_____

Red, White, Blush, Rose

Appellation _____

The specific area in the world the grapes were grown. (e.g., Barossa Valley, Marlborough, Napa Valley, Rhone).

Name/Winery_____

The brand name is usually the winery name. They may be different or the same.

Vineyard/Estate _____

Vintage/Year _____

All grapes in the bottle must have been grown in this year.

My Comments _____

_____

_____

_____

Will I Buy It? Yes _____ No _____ Price $ _____

Red Grape Variety	Common Sensory Descriptors
Cabernet Franc	tobacco, green bell pepper, raspberry, grass
Cabernet Sauvignon	blackcurrants, eucalyptus, chocolate, tobacco
Gamay	pomegranate, strawberry, red fruits
Grenache	smoky, pepper, raspberry
Malbec	violet, fruit, beer
Merlot	black cherry, plums, tomato
Mouvèdre	thyme, clove, cinnamon, pepper, violet, blackberry
Nebbiolo	leather, tar-stewed prunes, chocolate, liquorice, roses
Petite Sirah	earthy, black pepper, dark fruits
Petit Verdot	violets, pencil shavings
Pinot Noir	raspberry, cherry, violets, "farmyard" (with age) truffles
Pinotage	bramble fruits (blackberry, raspberry, loganberry)
Sangiovese	herbs, black cherry, leathery, earthy
Syrah(Shiraz)	tobacco black/white pepper, blackberry, smoke
Tempranillo	vanilla, strawberry, tobacco
Zinfandel	black cherry, pepper, mixed spices, mint

My Notes

Wine/Grape _____ (write in or circle below.)

White: Albariño, Chardonnay, Chenin Blanc, Gewürztraminer, Gruner Veltliner, Marsanne, Muscat, Palomino, Pinot Gris/ Grigio, Prosecco, Riesling, Sauvignon Blanc/Fume Blanc, Semillon, Trebbiano, Verdicchio, Viognier

Red: Cabernet Franc, Cabernet Sauvignon, Gamay, Grenache, Malbec, Merlot, Mourvèdre, Nebbiolo, Petite Verdot, Pinot Noir, Pinotage, Sangiovese, Syrah/Petite Sirah/Shiraz, Tempranillo, Zinfandel

Color _____

Red, White, Blush, Rose

Appellation _____

The specific area in the world the grapes were grown. (e.g., Barossa Valley, Marlborough, Napa Valley, Rhone).

Name/Winery _____

The brand name is usually the winery name. They may be different or the same.

Vineyard/Estate _____

Vintage/Year _____

All grapes in the bottle must have been grown in this year.

My Comments _____

_____

_____

_____

Will I Buy It? Yes ____ No ____ Price $ _____

White Grape Variety	Common Sensory Descriptors
Albariño	lemon, minerals
Chardonnay	butter, melon, apple, pineapple, vanilla, oaked (if vinified or aged in new oak barrels)
Chenin Blanc	wet wool, beeswax, honey, apple, almond
Gewürztraminer	rose petals, lychee, spice
Grüner Veltliner	green apple, citrus
Marsanne	almond, honeysuckle, marzipan
Muscat	honey, grapes, lime
Palomino	honeydew, citrus, raw nuts
Pinot Gris (Pinot Grigio)	white peach, pear, apricot
Prosecco	apple, honey, musk, citrus
Riesling	citrus fruits, peach, honey, petrol
Sauvignon Blanc	gooseberry, lime, asparagus, grass, bell pepper, grapefruit, cat pee
Sémillon	honey, orange, lime
Trebbiano (Ugni Blanc)	lime, herbs
Verdicchio	apple, minerals, citrus
Viognier	peach, pear, nutmeg, apricot

My Notes

Wine/Grape _____ (write in or circle below.)

White: Albariño, Chardonnay, Chenin Blanc, Gewürztraminer, Gruner Veltliner, Marsanne, Muscat, Palomino, Pinot Gris/Grigio, Prosecco, Riesling, Sauvignon Blanc/Fume Blanc, Semillon, Trebbiano, Verdicchio, Viognier

Red: Cabernet Franc, Cabernet Sauvignon, Gamay, Grenache, Malbec, Merlot, Mourvèdre, Nebbiolo, Petite Verdot, Pinot Noir, Pinotage, Sangiovese, Syrah/Petite Sirah/Shiraz, Tempranillo, Zinfandel

Color _____

Red, White, Blush, Rose

Appellation _____

The specific area in the world the grapes were grown. (e.g., Barossa Valley, Marlborough, Napa Valley, Rhone).

Name/Winery _____

The brand name is usually the winery name. They may be different or the same.

Vineyard/Estate _____

Vintage/Year _____

All grapes in the bottle must have been grown in this year.

My Comments _____

_____

_____

_____

Will I Buy It? Yes ____No ____ Price $ _____

Tip #1

Don't be afraid to ask for help choosing a wine at a retail store or restaurant.

My Notes

Wine/Grape _____ (write in or circle below.)

White: Albariño, Chardonnay, Chenin Blanc, Gewürztraminer, Gruner Veltliner, Marsanne, Muscat, Palomino, Pinot Gris/Grigio, Prosecco, Riesling, Sauvignon Blanc/Fume Blanc, Semillon, Trebbiano, Verdicchio, Viognier

Red: Cabernet Franc, Cabernet Sauvignon, Gamay, Grenache, Malbec, Merlot, Mourvèdre, Nebbiolo, Petite Verdot, Pinot Noir, Pinotage, Sangiovese, Syrah/Petite Sirah/Shiraz, Tempranillo, Zinfandel

Color _____

Red, White, Blush, Rose

Appellation _____

The specific area in the world the grapes were grown. (e.g., Barossa Valley, Marlborough, Napa Valley, Rhone).

Name/Winery _____

The brand name is usually the winery name. They may be different or the same.

Vineyard/Estate _____

Vintage/Year _____

All grapes in the bottle must have been grown in this year.

My Comments _____

_____

_____

_____

Will I Buy It? Yes ____ No ____ Price $ _____

Tip #2

Know your geography. The wine's appellation is the area of the world where the grapes were grown. Better wines come from better vineyards.

My Notes

Wine/Grape _____ (write in or circle below.)

White: Albariño, Chardonnay, Chenin Blanc, Gewürztraminer, Gruner Veltliner, Marsanne, Muscat, Palomino, Pinot Gris/Grigio, Prosecco, Riesling, Sauvignon Blanc/Fume Blanc, Semillon, Trebbiano, Verdicchio, Viognier

Red: Cabernet Franc, Cabernet Sauvignon, Gamay, Grenache, Malbec, Merlot, Mourvèdre, Nebbiolo, Petite Verdot, Pinot Noir, Pinotage, Sangiovese, Syrah/Petite Sirah/Shiraz, Tempranillo, Zinfandel

Color_____

Red, White, Blush, Rose

Appellation _____

The specific area in the world the grapes were grown. (e.g., Barossa Valley, Marlborough, Napa Valley, Rhone).

Name/Winery_____

The brand name is usually the winery name. They may be different or the same.

Vineyard/Estate _____

Vintage/Year _____

All grapes in the bottle must have been grown in this year.

My Comments _____

_____

_____

_____

Will I Buy It? Yes _____No _____ Price $ _____

Tip #3

Body describes the feel of a wine in the mouth, due mostly to alcohol and sweetness. Opposites: low alcohol wines (8 to 12%) usually feel light, crisp, and refreshing; high alcohol wines (13.5 to 15.5%) are often described as meaty, weighty, and full.

My Notes

Wine/Grape _____ (write in or circle below.)

White: Albariño, Chardonnay, Chenin Blanc, Gewürztraminer, Gruner Veltliner, Marsanne, Muscat, Palomino, Pinot Gris/Grigio, Prosecco, Riesling, Sauvignon Blanc/Fume Blanc, Semillon, Trebbiano, Verdicchio, Viognier

Red: Cabernet Franc, Cabernet Sauvignon, Gamay, Grenache, Malbec, Merlot, Mourvèdre, Nebbiolo, Petite Verdot, Pinot Noir, Pinotage, Sangiovese, Syrah/Petite Sirah/Shiraz, Tempranillo, Zinfandel

Color_____

Red, White, Blush, Rose

Appellation _____

The specific area in the world the grapes were grown. (e.g., Barossa Valley, Marlborough, Napa Valley, Rhone).

Name/Winery_____

The brand name is usually the winery name. They may be different or the same.

Vineyard/Estate _____

Vintage/Year _____

All grapes in the bottle must have been grown in this year.

My Comments _____

_____

_____

_____

Will I Buy It? Yes ____ No ____ Price $ _____

Tip #4

Check the vintage, which is the wine's "date of birth." Many of the wines made today are made to drink now, so drink up.

My Notes

Wine/Grape _____ (write in or circle below.)

White: Albariño, Chardonnay, Chenin Blanc, Gewürztraminer, Gruner Veltliner, Marsanne, Muscat, Palomino, Pinot Gris/Grigio, Prosecco, Riesling, Sauvignon Blanc/Fume Blanc, Semillon, Trebbiano, Verdicchio, Viognier

Red: Cabernet Franc, Cabernet Sauvignon, Gamay, Grenache, Malbec, Merlot, Mourvèdre, Nebbiolo, Petite Verdot, Pinot Noir, Pinotage, Sangiovese, Syrah/Petite Sirah/Shiraz, Tempranillo, Zinfandel

Color_____

Red, White, Blush, Rose

Appellation _____

The specific area in the world the grapes were grown. (e.g., Barossa Valley, Marlborough, Napa Valley, Rhone).

Name/Winery_____

The brand name is usually the winery name. They may be different or the same.

Vineyard/Estate _____

Vintage/Year _____

All grapes in the bottle must have been grown in this year.

My Comments _____

_____

_____

_____

Will I Buy It? Yes _____No _____ Price $ _____

Tip #5

To chill a white wine to proper serving temperature requires between 1 hour and 1½ hours in a refrigerator. Quicker (but harder to control): 15 to 20 minutes in a bucket of 1/3 ice, 2/3 water. To cool a red wine, 15 to 20 minutes in a refrigerator is enough. (If it's too cold, red wine often feels too astringent.)

My Notes

Wine/Grape _____ (write in or circle below.)

White: Albariño, Chardonnay, Chenin Blanc, Gewürztraminer, Gruner Veltliner, Marsanne, Muscat, Palomino, Pinot Gris/Grigio, Prosecco, Riesling, Sauvignon Blanc/Fume Blanc, Semillon, Trebbiano, Verdicchio, Viognier

Red: Cabernet Franc, Cabernet Sauvignon, Gamay, Grenache, Malbec, Merlot, Mourvèdre, Nebbiolo, Petite Verdot, Pinot Noir, Pinotage, Sangiovese, Syrah/Petite Sirah/Shiraz, Tempranillo, Zinfandel

Color _____

Red, White, Blush, Rose

Appellation _____

The specific area in the world the grapes were grown. (e.g., Barossa Valley, Marlborough, Napa Valley, Rhone).

Name/Winery _____

The brand name is usually the winery name. They may be different or the same.

Vineyard/Estate _____

Vintage/Year _____

All grapes in the bottle must have been grown in this year.

My Comments _____

_____

_____

_____

Will I Buy It? Yes ____ No ____ Price $ _____

Tip #6

Pay attention to the cork as you pull it. It should fit snugly, and not be stained with wine from bottom to top. Loose-fitting corks may have allowed too much air into the bottle, causing the wine to become sherried (oxidized). This is not only a sign of improper storage, but also equally possible, a sign of a poor-quality cork.

My Notes

Wine/Grape _____ (write in or circle below.)

White: Albariño, Chardonnay, Chenin Blanc, Gewürztraminer, Gruner Veltliner, Marsanne, Muscat, Palomino, Pinot Gris/Grigio, Prosecco, Riesling, Sauvignon Blanc/Fume Blanc, Semillon, Trebbiano, Verdicchio, Viognier

Red: Cabernet Franc, Cabernet Sauvignon, Gamay, Grenache, Malbec, Merlot, Mourvèdre, Nebbiolo, Petite Verdot, Pinot Noir, Pinotage, Sangiovese, Syrah/Petite Sirah/Shiraz, Tempranillo, Zinfandel

Color_____

Red, White, Blush, Rose

Appellation _____

The specific area in the world the grapes were grown. (e.g., Barossa Valley, Marlborough, Napa Valley, Rhone).

Name/Winery_____

The brand name is usually the winery name. They may be different or the same.

Vineyard/Estate _____

Vintage/Year _____

All grapes in the bottle must have been grown in this year.

My Comments _____

_____

_____

_____

Will I Buy It? Yes _____No _____ Price $ _____

Tip #7

Wine should smell and taste fresh of fruits or flowers when it is young. If it has been in the bottle for several years, it should smell more of spices, chocolate, or coffee as well as having souvenirs of its youth.

My Notes

Wine/Grape _____ (write in or circle below.)

White: Albariño, Chardonnay, Chenin Blanc, Gewürztraminer, Gruner Veltliner, Marsanne, Muscat, Palomino, Pinot Gris/Grigio, Prosecco, Riesling, Sauvignon Blanc/Fume Blanc, Semillon, Trebbiano, Verdicchio, Viognier

Red: Cabernet Franc, Cabernet Sauvignon, Gamay, Grenache, Malbec, Merlot, Mourvèdre, Nebbiolo, Petite Verdot, Pinot Noir, Pinotage, Sangiovese, Syrah/Petite Sirah/Shiraz, Tempranillo, Zinfandel

Color_____

Red, White, Blush, Rose

Appellation _____

The specific area in the world the grapes were grown. (e.g., Barossa Valley, Marlborough, Napa Valley, Rhone).

Name/Winery_____

The brand name is usually the winery name. They may be different or the same.

Vineyard/Estate _____

Vintage/Year _____

All grapes in the bottle must have been grown in this year.

My Comments _____

_____

_____

_____

Will I Buy It? Yes _____No _____ Price $ _____

Tip # 8

Your waiter should fill the glass 1/3 to 1/2 full so the wine can be swirled, allowing it to release its aromas and fragrances.

My Notes

Wine/Grape _____ (write in or circle below.)

White: Albariño, Chardonnay, Chenin Blanc, Gewürztraminer, Gruner Veltliner, Marsanne, Muscat, Palomino, Pinot Gris/Grigio, Prosecco, Riesling, Sauvignon Blanc/Fume Blanc, Semillon, Trebbiano, Verdicchio, Viognier

Red: Cabernet Franc, Cabernet Sauvignon, Gamay, Grenache, Malbec, Merlot, Mourvèdre, Nebbiolo, Petite Verdot, Pinot Noir, Pinotage, Sangiovese, Syrah/Petite Sirah/Shiraz, Tempranillo, Zinfandel

Color_____

Red, White, Blush, Rose

Appellation _____

The specific area in the world the grapes were grown. (e.g., Barossa Valley, Marlborough, Napa Valley, Rhone).

Name/Winery_____

The brand name is usually the winery name. They may be different or the same.

Vineyard/Estate _____

Vintage/Year _____

All grapes in the bottle must have been grown in this year.

My Comments _____

_____

_____

_____

Will I Buy It? Yes _____ No _____ Price $ _____

Tip # 9

Pay attention to the wine's temperature. White wine and champagne should be served chilled; reds are served at room temperature. Keep in mind that if a wine is too cold, this will disguise its flaws. It is perfectly acceptable to leave your bottle of white wine out of the bucket for 10–15 minutes to allow the wine to warm up if you think it's too cold. You may ask for an ice bucket if you believe your red wine is too warm. It's all about what *you* like.

My Notes

Wine/Grape _____ (write in or circle below.)

White: Albariño, Chardonnay, Chenin Blanc, Gewürztraminer, Gruner Veltliner, Marsanne, Muscat, Palomino, Pinot Gris/Grigio, Prosecco, Riesling, Sauvignon Blanc/Fume Blanc, Semillon, Trebbiano, Verdicchio, Viognier

Red: Cabernet Franc, Cabernet Sauvignon, Gamay, Grenache, Malbec, Merlot, Mourvèdre, Nebbiolo, Petite Verdot, Pinot Noir, Pinotage, Sangiovese, Syrah/Petite Sirah/Shiraz, Tempranillo, Zinfandel

Color_____

Red, White, Blush, Rose

Appellation _____

The specific area in the world the grapes were grown. (e.g., Barossa Valley, Marlborough, Napa Valley, Rhone).

Name/Winery_____

The brand name is usually the winery name. They may be different or the same.

Vineyard/Estate _____

Vintage/Year _____

All grapes in the bottle must have been grown in this year.

My Comments _____

_____

_____

_____

Will I Buy It? Yes _____ No _____ Price $ _____

Tip # 10

Please keep in mind that when you purchase wine at a restaurant, you are paying for service. Thus, it is customary for restaurants to charge 2 to 3 times the price you would pay at retail. Try enjoying a wine you don't know the price of and have not yet tasted. Initially you may be disappointed at the price you paid, and then you'll realize you can purchase the wine at much less and enjoy it at home with friends and family.

My Notes

Wine/Grape _____ (write in or circle below.)

White: Albariño, Chardonnay, Chenin Blanc, Gewürztraminer, Gruner Veltliner, Marsanne, Muscat, Palomino, Pinot Gris/Grigio, Prosecco, Riesling, Sauvignon Blanc/Fume Blanc, Semillon, Trebbiano, Verdicchio, Viognier

Red: Cabernet Franc, Cabernet Sauvignon, Gamay, Grenache, Malbec, Merlot, Mourvèdre, Nebbiolo, Petite Verdot, Pinot Noir, Pinotage, Sangiovese, Syrah/Petite Sirah/Shiraz, Tempranillo, Zinfandel

Color_____

Red, White, Blush, Rose

Appellation _____

The specific area in the world the grapes were grown. (e.g., Barossa Valley, Marlborough, Napa Valley, Rhone).

Name/Winery_____

The brand name is usually the winery name. They may be different or the same.

Vineyard/Estate _____

Vintage/Year _____

All grapes in the bottle must have been grown in this year.

My Comments _____

_____

_____

_____

Will I Buy It? Yes ____No ____ Price $ _____

Corks

Q: Why do they present the cork to you after the bottle is opened?

A: The cork is presented so you can ensure the winery name on the cork matches the name of the winery on the label. Many years ago some dishonest wine makers started putting copies of more expensive wine labels on their not-so-expensive wine. So, wineries began to place their names on the cork. Today, you can find a lot more information on a cork, including website and phone information. Fantesca Winery features "fortune corkies," which are wine quotes on their corks.

Q: What do I do with the cork when it's presented?

When a cork is presented to you, smell the cork. If it is infected with TCA (or 2,4,6-trichloroanisole) it will smell just as moldy/mildewed as the wine beneath it. A cork with wine marks from stem to stern or top to bottom may be an indication the bottle was not stored properly. Therefore, take special notice of what's in the glass when you stick your nose in it.

Q: Why we are seeing fewer bottles with corks and more with synthetic, stelvin, or screw caps?

When you think about it, using a cork to close a bottle of wine is an antiquated system. Sure, over time cork contributes some of its own chemical components to the flavor of the wine. But synthetics, especially screw caps, are more reliable closures, so they keep wines fresher and untainted by off-flavors. They are well-proven over the short term, and increasingly reliable for longer aging.

My Notes

Wine/Grape _____ (write in or circle below.)

White: Albariño, Chardonnay, Chenin Blanc, Gewürztraminer, Gruner Veltliner, Marsanne, Muscat, Palomino, Pinot Gris/Grigio, Prosecco, Riesling, Sauvignon Blanc/Fume Blanc, Semillon, Trebbiano, Verdicchio, Viognier

Red: Cabernet Franc, Cabernet Sauvignon, Gamay, Grenache, Malbec, Merlot, Mourvèdre, Nebbiolo, Petite Verdot, Pinot Noir, Pinotage, Sangiovese, Syrah/Petite Sirah/Shiraz, Tempranillo, Zinfandel

Color_____

Red, White, Blush, Rose

Appellation _____

The specific area in the world the grapes were grown. (e.g., Barossa Valley, Marlborough, Napa Valley, Rhone).

Name/Winery_____

The brand name is usually the winery name. They may be different or the same.

Vineyard/Estate _____

Vintage/Year _____

All grapes in the bottle must have been grown in this year.

My Comments _____

_____

_____

_____

Will I Buy It? Yes ____No ____Price $ _____

The Correct Temperature for Wine

The correct temperature allows the best of the wine to come through. However, the temperatures given here are to be used as a guide. If you like to drink your whites a little warmer or reds slightly chilled, by all means do so.

Place white wine in the refrigerator for 1 hour to 1½ hours to achieve proper serving temperature.

Place your red wines in the refrigerator for 15–20 minutes before serving.

Use an ice bucket with 1/3 ice and 2/3 water to chill a bottle of champagne, sparkling, or white wine quickly.

Cellar Temperature for All Wine

45°–55° Fahrenheit and humidity between
60%–70%.

Serving Temperature

60°F –65°F (15.5°C–18.3°C)

Full-bodied reds: Cabernet Sauvignon, Merlot, Shiraz, Syrah, Port.

50°F–60°F (10°C–15.5°C)

Light, fruity reds: Beaujolais, light Pinot Noir.

Full-bodied whites: Chardonnay, Viognier

45°F–50°F (7°C–10°C)

Champagne, sparkling wine, Sauvignon Blanc, Fume Blanc, Pinot Grigio, Riesling, Gewürztraminer.

Remember, your preference is most important!

My Notes

Wine/Grape _____ (write in or circle below.)

White: Albariño, Chardonnay, Chenin Blanc, Gewürztraminer, Gruner Veltliner, Marsanne, Muscat, Palomino, Pinot Gris/Grigio, Prosecco, Riesling, Sauvignon Blanc/Fume Blanc, Semillon, Trebbiano, Verdicchio, Viognier

Red: Cabernet Franc, Cabernet Sauvignon, Gamay, Grenache, Malbec, Merlot, Mourvèdre, Nebbiolo, Petite Verdot, Pinot Noir, Pinotage, Sangiovese, Syrah/Petite Sirah/Shiraz, Tempranillo, Zinfandel

Color_____

Red, White, Blush, Rose

Appellation _____

The specific area in the world the grapes were grown. (e.g., Barossa Valley, Marlborough, Napa Valley, Rhone).

Name/Winery_____

The brand name is usually the winery name. They may be different or the same.

Vineyard/Estate _____

Vintage/Year _____

All grapes in the bottle must have been grown in this year.

My Comments _____

_____
_____
_____

Will I Buy It? Yes ____No ____ Price $ _____

Serving Wine

Tip #1

White wine is usually served before red wine.

My Notes

Wine/Grape _____ (write in or circle below.)

White: Albariño, Chardonnay, Chenin Blanc, Gewürztraminer, Gruner Veltliner, Marsanne, Muscat, Palomino, Pinot Gris/Grigio, Prosecco, Riesling, Sauvignon Blanc/Fume Blanc, Semillon, Trebbiano, Verdicchio, Viognier

Red: Cabernet Franc, Cabernet Sauvignon, Gamay, Grenache, Malbec, Merlot, Mourvèdre, Nebbiolo, Petite Verdot, Pinot Noir, Pinotage, Sangiovese, Syrah/Petite Sirah/Shiraz, Tempranillo, Zinfandel

Color_____

Red, White, Blush, Rose

Appellation _____

The specific area in the world the grapes were grown. (e.g., Barossa Valley, Marlborough, Napa Valley, Rhone).

Name/Winery_____

The brand name is usually the winery name. They may be different or the same.

Vineyard/Estate _____

Vintage/Year _____

All grapes in the bottle must have been grown in this year.

My Comments _____

_____

_____

_____

Will I Buy It? Yes ____No ____Price $ _____

Serving Wine

Tip #2

Serve light-bodied wines before full-bodied wines.

My Notes

Wine/Grape _____ (write in or circle below.)

White: Albariño, Chardonnay, Chenin Blanc, Gewürztraminer, Gruner Veltliner, Marsanne, Muscat, Palomino, Pinot Gris/Grigio, Prosecco, Riesling, Sauvignon Blanc/Fume Blanc, Semillon, Trebbiano, Verdicchio, Viognier

Red: Cabernet Franc, Cabernet Sauvignon, Gamay, Grenache, Malbec, Merlot, Mourvèdre, Nebbiolo, Petite Verdot, Pinot Noir, Pinotage, Sangiovese, Syrah/Petite Sirah/Shiraz, Tempranillo, Zinfandel

Color_____

Red, White, Blush, Rose

Appellation _____

The specific area in the world the grapes were grown. (e.g., Barossa Valley, Marlborough, Napa Valley, Rhone).

Name/Winery_____

The brand name is usually the winery name. They may be different or the same.

Vineyard/Estate _____

Vintage/Year _____

All grapes in the bottle must have been grown in this year.

My Comments _____

_____

_____

_____

Will I Buy It? Yes ____No ____ Price $ _____

Serving Wine

Tip #3

Serve "good" wine before "great" wine.

My Notes

Wine/Grape _____ (write in or circle below.)

White: Albariño, Chardonnay, Chenin Blanc, Gewürztraminer, Gruner Veltliner, Marsanne, Muscat, Palomino, Pinot Gris/Grigio, Prosecco, Riesling, Sauvignon Blanc/Fume Blanc, Semillon, Trebbiano, Verdicchio, Viognier

Red: Cabernet Franc, Cabernet Sauvignon, Gamay, Grenache, Malbec, Merlot, Mourvèdre, Nebbiolo, Petite Verdot, Pinot Noir, Pinotage, Sangiovese, Syrah/Petite Sirah/Shiraz, Tempranillo, Zinfandel

Color_____

Red, White, Blush, Rose

Appellation _____

The specific area in the world the grapes were grown. (e.g., Barossa Valley, Marlborough, Napa Valley, Rhone).

Name/Winery_____

The brand name is usually the winery name. They may be different or the same.

Vineyard/Estate _____

Vintage/Year _____

All grapes in the bottle must have been grown in this year.

My Comments _____

_____

_____

_____

Will I Buy It? Yes ____No ____Price $ _____

Serving Wine

Tip #4

Serve younger wine before older wine.

My Notes

Wine/Grape _____ (write in or circle below.)

White: Albariño, Chardonnay, Chenin Blanc, Gewürztraminer, Gruner Veltliner, Marsanne, Muscat, Palomino, Pinot Gris/ Grigio, Prosecco, Riesling, Sauvignon Blanc/Fume Blanc, Semillon, Trebbiano, Verdicchio, Viognier

Red: Cabernet Franc, Cabernet Sauvignon, Gamay, Grenache, Malbec, Merlot, Mourvèdre, Nebbiolo, Petite Verdot, Pinot Noir, Pinotage, Sangiovese, Syrah/Petite Sirah/Shiraz, Tempranillo, Zinfandel

Color_____

Red, White, Blush, Rose

Appellation _____

The specific area in the world the grapes were grown. (e.g., Barossa Valley, Marlborough, Napa Valley, Rhone).

Name/Winery_____

The brand name is usually the winery name. They may be different or the same.

Vineyard/Estate _____

Vintage/Year _____

All grapes in the bottle must have been grown in this year.

My Comments _____

_____

_____

_____

Will I Buy It? Yes ____No ____ Price $ _____

Serving Wine

Tip #5

Serve dry wine before sweet wine.

My Notes

Wine/Grape _____ (write in or circle below.)

White: Albariño, Chardonnay, Chenin Blanc, Gewürztraminer, Gruner Veltliner, Marsanne, Muscat, Palomino, Pinot Gris/Grigio, Prosecco, Riesling, Sauvignon Blanc/Fume Blanc, Semillon, Trebbiano, Verdicchio, Viognier

Red: Cabernet Franc, Cabernet Sauvignon, Gamay, Grenache, Malbec, Merlot, Mourvèdre, Nebbiolo, Petite Verdot, Pinot Noir, Pinotage, Sangiovese, Syrah/Petite Sirah/Shiraz, Tempranillo, Zinfandel

Color _____

Red, White, Blush, Rose

Appellation _____

The specific area in the world the grapes were grown. (e.g., Barossa Valley, Marlborough, Napa Valley, Rhone).

Name/Winery _____

The brand name is usually the winery name. They may be different or the same.

Vineyard/Estate _____

Vintage/Year _____

All grapes in the bottle must have been grown in this year.

My Comments _____

_____

_____

_____

Will I Buy It? Yes ____ No ____ Price $ _____

Serving Wine

Tip #6

Serve light-bodied wine with lighter meals, full-bodied wine with richer dishes.

My Notes

Wine/Grape _____ (write in or circle below.)

White: Albariño, Chardonnay, Chenin Blanc, Gewürztraminer, Gruner Veltliner, Marsanne, Muscat, Palomino, Pinot Gris/Grigio, Prosecco, Riesling, Sauvignon Blanc/Fume Blanc, Semillon, Trebbiano, Verdicchio, Viognier

Red: Cabernet Franc, Cabernet Sauvignon, Gamay, Grenache, Malbec, Merlot, Mourvèdre, Nebbiolo, Petite Verdot, Pinot Noir, Pinotage, Sangiovese, Syrah/Petite Sirah/Shiraz, Tempranillo, Zinfandel

Color _____

Red, White, Blush, Rose

Appellation _____

The specific area in the world the grapes were grown. (e.g., Barossa Valley, Marlborough, Napa Valley, Rhone).

Name/Winery _____

The brand name is usually the winery name. They may be different or the same.

Vineyard/Estate _____

Vintage/Year _____

All grapes in the bottle must have been grown in this year.

My Comments _____

_____

_____

_____

Will I Buy It? Yes _____ No _____ Price $ _____

Serving Wine

Tip #7

Serve white wine with fish, chicken, and light sauces.

My Notes

Wine/Grape _____ (write in or circle below.)

White: Albariño, Chardonnay, Chenin Blanc, Gewürztraminer, Gruner Veltliner, Marsanne, Muscat, Palomino, Pinot Gris/Grigio, Prosecco, Riesling, Sauvignon Blanc/Fume Blanc, Semillon, Trebbiano, Verdicchio, Viognier

Red: Cabernet Franc, Cabernet Sauvignon, Gamay, Grenache, Malbec, Merlot, Mourvèdre, Nebbiolo, Petite Verdot, Pinot Noir, Pinotage, Sangiovese, Syrah/Petite Sirah/Shiraz, Tempranillo, Zinfandel

Color_____

Red, White, Blush, Rose

Appellation _____

The specific area in the world the grapes were grown. (e.g., Barossa Valley, Marlborough, Napa Valley, Rhone).

Name/Winery_____

The brand name is usually the winery name. They may be different or the same.

Vineyard/Estate _____

Vintage/Year _____

All grapes in the bottle must have been grown in this year.

My Comments _____

_____

_____

_____

Will I Buy It? Yes ____No ____ Price $ _____

Serving Wine

Tip #8

Serve red wine with red meats, stews, pizza, and salmon.

My Notes

Wine/Grape _____ (write in or circle below.)

White: Albariño, Chardonnay, Chenin Blanc, Gewürztraminer, Gruner Veltliner, Marsanne, Muscat, Palomino, Pinot Gris/Grigio, Prosecco, Riesling, Sauvignon Blanc/Fume Blanc, Semillon, Trebbiano, Verdicchio, Viognier

Red: Cabernet Franc, Cabernet Sauvignon, Gamay, Grenache, Malbec, Merlot, Mourvèdre, Nebbiolo, Petite Verdot, Pinot Noir, Pinotage, Sangiovese, Syrah/Petite Sirah/Shiraz, Tempranillo, Zinfandel

Color_____

Red, White, Blush, Rose

Appellation _____

The specific area in the world the grapes were grown. (e.g., Barossa Valley, Marlborough, Napa Valley, Rhone).

Name/Winery_____

The brand name is usually the winery name. They may be different or the same.

Vineyard/Estate _____

Vintage/Year _____

All grapes in the bottle must have been grown in this year.

My Comments _____

_____

_____

_____

Will I Buy It? Yes ____No ____ Price $ _____

Serving Wine

Tip #9

If the food you're serving was prepared with wine, serve the same wine you used for cooking.

My Notes

Wine/Grape _____ (write in or circle below.)

White: Albariño, Chardonnay, Chenin Blanc, Gewürztraminer, Gruner Veltliner, Marsanne, Muscat, Palomino, Pinot Gris/Grigio, Prosecco, Riesling, Sauvignon Blanc/Fume Blanc, Semillon, Trebbiano, Verdicchio, Viognier

Red: Cabernet Franc, Cabernet Sauvignon, Gamay, Grenache, Malbec, Merlot, Mourvèdre, Nebbiolo, Petite Verdot, Pinot Noir, Pinotage, Sangiovese, Syrah/Petite Sirah/Shiraz, Tempranillo, Zinfandel

Color_____

Red, White, Blush, Rose

Appellation _____

The specific area in the world the grapes were grown. (e.g., Barossa Valley, Marlborough, Napa Valley, Rhone).

Name/Winery_____

The brand name is usually the winery name. They may be different or the same.

Vineyard/Estate _____

Vintage/Year _____

All grapes in the bottle must have been grown in this year.

My Comments _____

_____

_____

_____

Will I Buy It? Yes ____ No ____ Price $ _____

Serving Wine

Tip #10

If you would not drink a wine, do not use it for cooking. The characteristics you don't like will come out in your dish.

My Notes

Wine/Grape _____ (write in or circle below.)

White: Albariño, Chardonnay, Chenin Blanc, Gewürztraminer, Gruner Veltliner, Marsanne, Muscat, Palomino, Pinot Gris/Grigio, Prosecco, Riesling, Sauvignon Blanc/Fume Blanc, Semillon, Trebbiano, Verdicchio, Viognier

Red: Cabernet Franc, Cabernet Sauvignon, Gamay, Grenache, Malbec, Merlot, Mourvèdre, Nebbiolo, Petite Verdot, Pinot Noir, Pinotage, Sangiovese, Syrah/Petite Sirah/Shiraz, Tempranillo, Zinfandel

Color_____

Red, White, Blush, Rose

Appellation _____

The specific area in the world the grapes were grown. (e.g., Barossa Valley, Marlborough, Napa Valley, Rhone).

Name/Winery_____

The brand name is usually the winery name. They may be different or the same.

Vineyard/Estate _____

Vintage/Year _____

All grapes in the bottle must have been grown in this year.

My Comments_____

_____

_____

_____

Will I Buy It? Yes _____No _____ Price $ _____

Serving Wine

Tip #11

When serving sauces, look for a wine that has characteristics similar to the sauces you are serving.

My Notes

Wine/Grape _____ (write in or circle below.)

White: Albariño, Chardonnay, Chenin Blanc, Gewürztraminer, Gruner Veltliner, Marsanne, Muscat, Palomino, Pinot Gris/Grigio, Prosecco, Riesling, Sauvignon Blanc/Fume Blanc, Semillon, Trebbiano, Verdicchio, Viognier

Red: Cabernet Franc, Cabernet Sauvignon, Gamay, Grenache, Malbec, Merlot, Mourvèdre, Nebbiolo, Petite Verdot, Pinot Noir, Pinotage, Sangiovese, Syrah/Petite Sirah/Shiraz, Tempranillo, Zinfandel

Color_____

Red, White, Blush, Rose

Appellation _____

The specific area in the world the grapes were grown. (e.g., Barossa Valley, Marlborough, Napa Valley, Rhone).

Name/Winery_____

The brand name is usually the winery name. They may be different or the same.

Vineyard/Estate _____

Vintage/Year _____

All grapes in the bottle must have been grown in this year.

My Comments _____

_____

_____

_____

Will I Buy It? Yes _____ No _____ Price $ _____

Decanting Wine

Decanting is the process of pouring or transferring a bottle of wine into a clear clean serving container.

Older wines may develop sediment at the bottom of the bottle as they age. Decanting the wine allows separation of the drinkable wine from the sediment. Pour the wine slowly to avoid transferring the sediment into the decanter. (The sediment is not harmful.) Decanting an older wine allows air into the wine, bringing out the aroma and fragrances.

Many of the wines we drink today are released before aging. Decanting younger wines several hours before serving helps them to evolve quickly, due to the infusion of air they receive in the process. If you don't have a decanter, pour the wine into wine glasses 15–20 minutes before your guests arrive.

Remember, the primary purpose of decanting is to let air into the wine, allowing it to breathe. Removing the cork and letting the bottle sit without decanting or pouring it into glasses does not let sufficient air into the bottle.

My Notes

Wine/Grape _____ (write in or circle below.)

White: Albariño, Chardonnay, Chenin Blanc, Gewürztraminer, Gruner Veltliner, Marsanne, Muscat, Palomino, Pinot Gris/Grigio, Prosecco, Riesling, Sauvignon Blanc/Fume Blanc, Semillon, Trebbiano, Verdicchio, Viognier

Red: Cabernet Franc, Cabernet Sauvignon, Gamay, Grenache, Malbec, Merlot, Mourvèdre, Nebbiolo, Petite Verdot, Pinot Noir, Pinotage, Sangiovese, Syrah/Petite Sirah/Shiraz, Tempranillo, Zinfandel

Color_____

Red, White, Blush, Rose

Appellation _____

The specific area in the world the grapes were grown. (e.g., Barossa Valley, Marlborough, Napa Valley, Rhone).

Name/Winery_____

The brand name is usually the winery name. They may be different or the same.

Vineyard/Estate _____

Vintage/Year _____

All grapes in the bottle must have been grown in this year.

My Comments _____

_____

_____

_____

Will I Buy It? Yes ____No ____ Price $ _____

"Wine is like life; sometimes it's not so easy to take, other times it's like you're in heaven."

—Author Unknown

My Notes

Wine/Grape _____ (write in or circle below.)

White: Albariño, Chardonnay, Chenin Blanc, Gewürztraminer, Gruner Veltliner, Marsanne, Muscat, Palomino, Pinot Gris/Grigio, Prosecco, Riesling, Sauvignon Blanc/Fume Blanc, Semillon, Trebbiano, Verdicchio, Viognier

Red: Cabernet Franc, Cabernet Sauvignon, Gamay, Grenache, Malbec, Merlot, Mourvèdre, Nebbiolo, Petite Verdot, Pinot Noir, Pinotage, Sangiovese, Syrah/Petite Sirah/Shiraz, Tempranillo, Zinfandel

Color_____

Red, White, Blush, Rose

Appellation _____

The specific area in the world the grapes were grown. (e.g., Barossa Valley, Marlborough, Napa Valley, Rhone).

Name/Winery_____

The brand name is usually the winery name. They may be different or the same.

Vineyard/Estate _____

Vintage/Year _____

All grapes in the bottle must have been grown in this year.

My Comments _____

_____

_____

_____

Will I Buy It? Yes ____No ____ Price $ _____

Opening a Bottle of Wine

I began opening bottles of wine with a handheld corkscrew (or waiter's corkscrew) and continue to use one today.

Don't be afraid of the wine bottle. Grip it firmly in your hand.

The first step is to remove enough of the metal/plastic capsule (commonly referred to as the foil) so the wine will not touch it when you pour. The foil was originally made of lead. The lead was thought to impart a metallic taste to the wine if the wine came in contact with it. Today, we don't need to worry about that because they no longer use lead to make the capsule. But it makes for a nicer presentation of the bottle to cut the foil. Use the knife on the end of the corkscrew or a foil cutter specially designed to make a nice clean cut.

When using a waiter's corkscrew:

1. Hold your wine opener straight and twist the corkscrew into the center of the cork, turning clockwise, taking care not to go all the way through the cork.

2. Attach the lever of your corkscrew to the edge of the bottle and use a slow steady pull to remove the cork.

There is nothing wrong with using rabbit ears; they are a little more difficult to take on a picnic but work just as well. You just need to open the bottle of wine!

My Notes

Wine/Grape _____ (write in or circle below.)

White: Albariño, Chardonnay, Chenin Blanc, Gewürztraminer, Gruner Veltliner, Marsanne, Muscat, Palomino, Pinot Gris/Grigio, Prosecco, Riesling, Sauvignon Blanc/Fume Blanc, Semillon, Trebbiano, Verdicchio, Viognier

Red: Cabernet Franc, Cabernet Sauvignon, Gamay, Grenache, Malbec, Merlot, Mourvèdre, Nebbiolo, Petite Verdot, Pinot Noir, Pinotage, Sangiovese, Syrah/Petite Sirah/Shiraz, Tempranillo, Zinfandel

Color_____

Red, White, Blush, Rose

Appellation _____

The specific area in the world the grapes were grown. (e.g., Barossa Valley, Marlborough, Napa Valley, Rhone).

Name/Winery_____

The brand name is usually the winery name. They may be different or the same.

Vineyard/Estate _____

Vintage/Year _____

All grapes in the bottle must have been grown in this year.

My Comments _____

_____

_____

_____

Will I Buy It? Yes ____No ____ Price $ _____

Glassware

As you already know, there are many different types of wine glasses, from the very expensive (Riedel) to old juice glasses like the ones my grandfather served his wine in.

If your budget only allows you to purchase one type of glass, I suggest what is known as the universal wine glass. It is acceptable when serving both red and white wines. As your pallet improves and your budget increases, you may want to consider purchasing more expensive glassware.

The first step in the Five S's is SEE, so you'll want to be sure your wine glasses are made of clear glass. My grandmother had the most beautiful set of pink wine glasses, which are great when serving red wine because they help enhance the color. Serving white wine in them makes the wine look green.

Wine glasses traditionally have a stem. This is to allow the drinker to hold the glass by the stem vs. the bowl of the glass. It helps keep the bowl clear so you can see the wine, and it keeps the heat from your hands from warming the wine.

Step number 2 is SWIRL. You will want glasses with a bowl large enough to allow you to swirl the wine without spilling and so you can get your nose into the glass when you move on to step number 3: SMELL.

My Notes

Wine/Grape _____ (write in or circle below.)

White: Albariño, Chardonnay, Chenin Blanc, Gewürztraminer, Gruner Veltliner, Marsanne, Muscat, Palomino, Pinot Gris/Grigio, Prosecco, Riesling, Sauvignon Blanc/Fume Blanc, Semillon, Trebbiano, Verdicchio, Viognier

Red: Cabernet Franc, Cabernet Sauvignon, Gamay, Grenache, Malbec, Merlot, Mourvèdre, Nebbiolo, Petite Verdot, Pinot Noir, Pinotage, Sangiovese, Syrah/Petite Sirah/Shiraz, Tempranillo, Zinfandel

Color_____

Red, White, Blush, Rose

Appellation _____

The specific area in the world the grapes were grown. (e.g., Barossa Valley, Marlborough, Napa Valley, Rhone).

Name/Winery_____

The brand name is usually the winery name. They may be different or the same.

Vineyard/Estate _____

Vintage/Year _____

All grapes in the bottle must have been grown in this year.

My Comments _____

_____

_____

_____

Will I Buy It? Yes _____No _____ Price $ _____

Food and Wine Pairing

L ike wine drinking, the most important thing with food and wine pairing is to eat and drink what you like.

There is no absolute rule to food and wine pairing; these are merely suggestions. You'll need to try a few wines and dishes together to determine your preference.

First think about what you are going to be eating, keeping in mind any sauces, salsas, and side you might be serving with your protein.

Red wine helps break down the protein in red meats, which in turn soften the tannins in the wine.

The tannins in red wine can make seafood taste metallic, one of the main reasons white wine is suggested with seafood.

Food dishes, like wines, also have characteristics. Steaks, pork chops, lamb, roasts are full bodied; they fill our mouths. Chicken and dense seafood, like salmon, tend to fall into the medium-body range while most other seafood is lighter in texture or body.

You'll want to match the body of the wine with the body of the food. A light seafood dish sprinkled with lemon will go well with Sauvignon Blanc or pinot grigio.

Serving a dish with a cherry fruit sauce will go well with Cabernet Sauvignon or Shirazes with hints of black cherry, cranberry or cherries on the nose and palette.

My Notes

Wine/Grape _____ (write in or circle below.)

White: Albariño, Chardonnay, Chenin Blanc, Gewürztraminer, Gruner Veltliner, Marsanne, Muscat, Palomino, Pinot Gris/Grigio, Prosecco, Riesling, Sauvignon Blanc/Fume Blanc, Semillon, Trebbiano, Verdicchio, Viognier

Red: Cabernet Franc, Cabernet Sauvignon, Gamay, Grenache, Malbec, Merlot, Mourvèdre, Nebbiolo, Petite Verdot, Pinot Noir, Pinotage, Sangiovese, Syrah/Petite Sirah/Shiraz, Tempranillo, Zinfandel

Color_____

Red, White, Blush, Rose

Appellation _____

The specific area in the world the grapes were grown. (e.g., Barossa Valley, Marlborough, Napa Valley, Rhone).

Name/Winery_____

The brand name is usually the winery name. They may be different or the same.

Vineyard/Estate _____

Vintage/Year _____

All grapes in the bottle must have been grown in this year.

My Comments _____

_____

_____

_____

Will I Buy It? Yes _____No _____ Price $ _____

Food and Wine Pairing (continued)

Foods either salty or sour can make wine seem fruitier and less acidic. Sweet and savory dishes may make the wine taste drier and appear more astringent.

Another way to look at food and wine pairing is to go for contrast. Spicy foods with sweet wines work well because the sweetness in the wine tames the spicy dish, allowing you to taste the food and taste the wine.

In the end, what you are looking for is a teeter-totter effect. You want to drink a wine that makes you want to take a bite of the food and then go back to the wine.

My Notes

Wine/Grape _____ (write in or circle below.)

White: Albariño, Chardonnay, Chenin Blanc, Gewürztraminer, Gruner Veltliner, Marsanne, Muscat, Palomino, Pinot Gris/Grigio, Prosecco, Riesling, Sauvignon Blanc/Fume Blanc, Semillon, Trebbiano, Verdicchio, Viognier

Red: Cabernet Franc, Cabernet Sauvignon, Gamay, Grenache, Malbec, Merlot, Mourvèdre, Nebbiolo, Petite Verdot, Pinot Noir, Pinotage, Sangiovese, Syrah/Petite Sirah/Shiraz, Tempranillo, Zinfandel

Color_____

Red, White, Blush, Rose

Appellation _____

The specific area in the world the grapes were grown. (e.g., Barossa Valley, Marlborough, Napa Valley, Rhone).

Name/Winery_____

The brand name is usually the winery name. They may be different or the same.

Vineyard/Estate _____

Vintage/Year _____

All grapes in the bottle must have been grown in this year.

My Comments _____

_____

_____

_____

Will I Buy It? Yes _____ No _____ Price $ _____

My Notes

Wine/Grape _____ (write in or circle below.)

White: Albariño, Chardonnay, Chenin Blanc, Gewürztraminer, Gruner Veltliner, Marsanne, Muscat, Palomino, Pinot Gris/Grigio, Prosecco, Riesling, Sauvignon Blanc/Fume Blanc, Semillon, Trebbiano, Verdicchio, Viognier

Red: Cabernet Franc, Cabernet Sauvignon, Gamay, Grenache, Malbec, Merlot, Mourvèdre, Nebbiolo, Petite Verdot, Pinot Noir, Pinotage, Sangiovese, Syrah/Petite Sirah/Shiraz, Tempranillo, Zinfandel

Color_____

Red, White, Blush, Rose

Appellation _____

The specific area in the world the grapes were grown. (e.g., Barossa Valley, Marlborough, Napa Valley, Rhone).

Name/Winery_____

The brand name is usually the winery name. They may be different or the same.

Vineyard/Estate _____

Vintage/Year _____

All grapes in the bottle must have been grown in this year.

My Comments _____

_____

_____

_____

Will I Buy It? Yes ____No ____Price $ _____

My Notes

Wine/Grape _____ (write in or circle below.)

White: Albariño, Chardonnay, Chenin Blanc, Gewürztraminer, Gruner Veltliner, Marsanne, Muscat, Palomino, Pinot Gris/Grigio, Prosecco, Riesling, Sauvignon Blanc/Fume Blanc, Semillon, Trebbiano, Verdicchio, Viognier

Red: Cabernet Franc, Cabernet Sauvignon, Gamay, Grenache, Malbec, Merlot, Mourvèdre, Nebbiolo, Petite Verdot, Pinot Noir, Pinotage, Sangiovese, Syrah/Petite Sirah/Shiraz, Tempranillo, Zinfandel

Color_____

Red, White, Blush, Rose

Appellation _____

The specific area in the world the grapes were grown. (e.g., Barossa Valley, Marlborough, Napa Valley, Rhone).

Name/Winery_____

The brand name is usually the winery name. They may be different or the same.

Vineyard/Estate _____

Vintage/Year _____

All grapes in the bottle must have been grown in this year.

My Comments _____

_____

_____

_____

Will I Buy It? Yes ____No ____Price $ _____

My Notes

Wine/Grape _____ (write in or circle below.)

White: Albariño, Chardonnay, Chenin Blanc, Gewürztraminer, Gruner Veltliner, Marsanne, Muscat, Palomino, Pinot Gris/Grigio, Prosecco, Riesling, Sauvignon Blanc/Fume Blanc, Semillon, Trebbiano, Verdicchio, Viognier

Red: Cabernet Franc, Cabernet Sauvignon, Gamay, Grenache, Malbec, Merlot, Mourvèdre, Nebbiolo, Petite Verdot, Pinot Noir, Pinotage, Sangiovese, Syrah/Petite Sirah/Shiraz, Tempranillo, Zinfandel

Color_____

Red, White, Blush, Rose

Appellation _____

The specific area in the world the grapes were grown. (e.g., Barossa Valley, Marlborough, Napa Valley, Rhone).

Name/Winery_____

The brand name is usually the winery name. They may be different or the same.

Vineyard/Estate _____

Vintage/Year _____

All grapes in the bottle must have been grown in this year.

My Comments _____

_____

_____

_____

Will I Buy It? Yes ____No ____Price $ _____

My Notes

Wine/Grape _____ (write in or circle below.)

White: Albariño, Chardonnay, Chenin Blanc, Gewürztraminer, Gruner Veltliner, Marsanne, Muscat, Palomino, Pinot Gris/Grigio, Prosecco, Riesling, Sauvignon Blanc/Fume Blanc, Semillon, Trebbiano, Verdicchio, Viognier

Red: Cabernet Franc, Cabernet Sauvignon, Gamay, Grenache, Malbec, Merlot, Mourvèdre, Nebbiolo, Petite Verdot, Pinot Noir, Pinotage, Sangiovese, Syrah/Petite Sirah/Shiraz, Tempranillo, Zinfandel

Color_____

Red, White, Blush, Rose

Appellation _____

The specific area in the world the grapes were grown. (e.g., Barossa Valley, Marlborough, Napa Valley, Rhone).

Name/Winery_____

The brand name is usually the winery name. They may be different or the same.

Vineyard/Estate _____

Vintage/Year _____

All grapes in the bottle must have been grown in this year.

My Comments _____

_____

_____

_____

Will I Buy It? Yes _____No _____ Price $ _____

My Notes

Wine/Grape _____ (write in or circle below.)

White: Albariño, Chardonnay, Chenin Blanc, Gewürztraminer, Gruner Veltliner, Marsanne, Muscat, Palomino, Pinot Gris/ Grigio, Prosecco, Riesling, Sauvignon Blanc/Fume Blanc, Semillon, Trebbiano, Verdicchio, Viognier

Red: Cabernet Franc, Cabernet Sauvignon, Gamay, Grenache, Malbec, Merlot, Mourvèdre, Nebbiolo, Petite Verdot, Pinot Noir, Pinotage, Sangiovese, Syrah/Petite Sirah/Shiraz, Tempranillo, Zinfandel

Color_____

Red, White, Blush, Rose

Appellation _____

The specific area in the world the grapes were grown. (e.g., Barossa Valley, Marlborough, Napa Valley, Rhone).

Name/Winery_____

The brand name is usually the winery name. They may be different or the same.

Vineyard/Estate _____

Vintage/Year _____

All grapes in the bottle must have been grown in this year.

My Comments _____

_____

_____

_____

Will I Buy It? Yes ____No ____Price $ _____

My Notes

Wine/Grape _____ (write in or circle below.)

White: Albariño, Chardonnay, Chenin Blanc, Gewürztraminer, Gruner Veltliner, Marsanne, Muscat, Palomino, Pinot Gris/Grigio, Prosecco, Riesling, Sauvignon Blanc/Fume Blanc, Semillon, Trebbiano, Verdicchio, Viognier

Red: Cabernet Franc, Cabernet Sauvignon, Gamay, Grenache, Malbec, Merlot, Mourvèdre, Nebbiolo, Petite Verdot, Pinot Noir, Pinotage, Sangiovese, Syrah/Petite Sirah/Shiraz, Tempranillo, Zinfandel

Color_____
Red, White, Blush, Rose

Appellation _____
The specific area in the world the grapes were grown. (e.g., Barossa Valley, Marlborough, Napa Valley, Rhone).

Name/Winery_____
The brand name is usually the winery name. They may be different or the same.

Vineyard/Estate _____

Vintage/Year _____
All grapes in the bottle must have been grown in this year.

My Comments _____

_____

_____

_____

Will I Buy It? Yes ____No ____ Price $ _____

My Notes

Wine/Grape _____ (write in or circle below.)

White: Albariño, Chardonnay, Chenin Blanc, Gewürztraminer, Gruner Veltliner, Marsanne, Muscat, Palomino, Pinot Gris/Grigio, Prosecco, Riesling, Sauvignon Blanc/Fume Blanc, Semillon, Trebbiano, Verdicchio, Viognier

Red: Cabernet Franc, Cabernet Sauvignon, Gamay, Grenache, Malbec, Merlot, Mourvèdre, Nebbiolo, Petite Verdot, Pinot Noir, Pinotage, Sangiovese, Syrah/Petite Sirah/Shiraz, Tempranillo, Zinfandel

Color_____

Red, White, Blush, Rose

Appellation _____

The specific area in the world the grapes were grown. (e.g., Barossa Valley, Marlborough, Napa Valley, Rhone).

Name/Winery_____

The brand name is usually the winery name. They may be different or the same.

Vineyard/Estate _____

Vintage/Year _____

All grapes in the bottle must have been grown in this year.

My Comments _____

_____

_____

_____

Will I Buy It? Yes ____No ____ Price $ _____

My Notes

Wine/Grape _____ (write in or circle below.)

White: Albariño, Chardonnay, Chenin Blanc, Gewürztraminer, Gruner Veltliner, Marsanne, Muscat, Palomino, Pinot Gris/Grigio, Prosecco, Riesling, Sauvignon Blanc/Fume Blanc, Semillon, Trebbiano, Verdicchio, Viognier

Red: Cabernet Franc, Cabernet Sauvignon, Gamay, Grenache, Malbec, Merlot, Mourvèdre, Nebbiolo, Petite Verdot, Pinot Noir, Pinotage, Sangiovese, Syrah/Petite Sirah/Shiraz, Tempranillo, Zinfandel

Color_____

Red, White, Blush, Rose

Appellation _____

The specific area in the world the grapes were grown. (e.g., Barossa Valley, Marlborough, Napa Valley, Rhone).

Name/Winery_____

The brand name is usually the winery name. They may be different or the same.

Vineyard/Estate _____

Vintage/Year _____

All grapes in the bottle must have been grown in this year.

My Comments _____

_____

_____

_____

Will I Buy It? Yes _____ No _____ Price $ _____

My Notes

Wine/Grape _____ (write in or circle below.)

White: Albariño, Chardonnay, Chenin Blanc, Gewürztraminer, Gruner Veltliner, Marsanne, Muscat, Palomino, Pinot Gris/Grigio, Prosecco, Riesling, Sauvignon Blanc/Fume Blanc, Semillon, Trebbiano, Verdicchio, Viognier

Red: Cabernet Franc, Cabernet Sauvignon, Gamay, Grenache, Malbec, Merlot, Mourvèdre, Nebbiolo, Petite Verdot, Pinot Noir, Pinotage, Sangiovese, Syrah/Petite Sirah/Shiraz, Tempranillo, Zinfandel

Color_____

Red, White, Blush, Rose

Appellation _____

The specific area in the world the grapes were grown. (e.g., Barossa Valley, Marlborough, Napa Valley, Rhone).

Name/Winery_____

The brand name is usually the winery name. They may be different or the same.

Vineyard/Estate _____

Vintage/Year _____

All grapes in the bottle must have been grown in this year.

My Comments _____

_____

_____

_____

Will I Buy It? Yes ____No ____Price $ _____

My Notes

Wine/Grape _____ (write in or circle below.)

White: Albariño, Chardonnay, Chenin Blanc, Gewürztraminer, Gruner Veltliner, Marsanne, Muscat, Palomino, Pinot Gris/Grigio, Prosecco, Riesling, Sauvignon Blanc/Fume Blanc, Semillon, Trebbiano, Verdicchio, Viognier

Red: Cabernet Franc, Cabernet Sauvignon, Gamay, Grenache, Malbec, Merlot, Mourvèdre, Nebbiolo, Petite Verdot, Pinot Noir, Pinotage, Sangiovese, Syrah/Petite Sirah/Shiraz, Tempranillo, Zinfandel

Color_____

Red, White, Blush, Rose

Appellation _____

The specific area in the world the grapes were grown. (e.g., Barossa Valley, Marlborough, Napa Valley, Rhone).

Name/Winery_____

The brand name is usually the winery name. They may be different or the same.

Vineyard/Estate _____

Vintage/Year _____

All grapes in the bottle must have been grown in this year.

My Comments _____

_____

_____

_____

Will I Buy It? Yes ____No ____ Price $ _____

My Notes

Wine/Grape _____ (write in or circle below.)

White: Albariño, Chardonnay, Chenin Blanc, Gewürztraminer, Gruner Veltliner, Marsanne, Muscat, Palomino, Pinot Gris/Grigio, Prosecco, Riesling, Sauvignon Blanc/Fume Blanc, Semillon, Trebbiano, Verdicchio, Viognier

Red: Cabernet Franc, Cabernet Sauvignon, Gamay, Grenache, Malbec, Merlot, Mourvèdre, Nebbiolo, Petite Verdot, Pinot Noir, Pinotage, Sangiovese, Syrah/Petite Sirah/Shiraz, Tempranillo, Zinfandel

Color_____

Red, White, Blush, Rose

Appellation _____

The specific area in the world the grapes were grown. (e.g., Barossa Valley, Marlborough, Napa Valley, Rhone).

Name/Winery_____

The brand name is usually the winery name. They may be different or the same.

Vineyard/Estate _____

Vintage/Year _____

All grapes in the bottle must have been grown in this year.

My Comments _____

_____

_____

_____

Will I Buy It? Yes _____ No _____ Price $ _____

My Notes

Wine/Grape _____ (write in or circle below.)

White: Albariño, Chardonnay, Chenin Blanc, Gewürztraminer, Gruner Veltliner, Marsanne, Muscat, Palomino, Pinot Gris/Grigio, Prosecco, Riesling, Sauvignon Blanc/Fume Blanc, Semillon, Trebbiano, Verdicchio, Viognier

Red: Cabernet Franc, Cabernet Sauvignon, Gamay, Grenache, Malbec, Merlot, Mourvèdre, Nebbiolo, Petite Verdot, Pinot Noir, Pinotage, Sangiovese, Syrah/Petite Sirah/Shiraz, Tempranillo, Zinfandel

Color_____

Red, White, Blush, Rose

Appellation _____

The specific area in the world the grapes were grown. (e.g., Barossa Valley, Marlborough, Napa Valley, Rhone).

Name/Winery_____

The brand name is usually the winery name. They may be different or the same.

Vineyard/Estate _____

Vintage/Year _____

All grapes in the bottle must have been grown in this year.

My Comments _____

_____

_____

_____

Will I Buy It? Yes ____No ____ Price $ _____

My Notes

Wine/Grape _____ (write in or circle below.)

White: Albariño, Chardonnay, Chenin Blanc, Gewürztraminer, Gruner Veltliner, Marsanne, Muscat, Palomino, Pinot Gris/Grigio, Prosecco, Riesling, Sauvignon Blanc/Fume Blanc, Semillon, Trebbiano, Verdicchio, Viognier

Red: Cabernet Franc, Cabernet Sauvignon, Gamay, Grenache, Malbec, Merlot, Mourvèdre, Nebbiolo, Petite Verdot, Pinot Noir, Pinotage, Sangiovese, Syrah/Petite Sirah/Shiraz, Tempranillo, Zinfandel

Color_____

Red, White, Blush, Rose

Appellation _____

The specific area in the world the grapes were grown. (e.g., Barossa Valley, Marlborough, Napa Valley, Rhone).

Name/Winery_____

The brand name is usually the winery name. They may be different or the same.

Vineyard/Estate _____

Vintage/Year _____

All grapes in the bottle must have been grown in this year.

My Comments _____

_____

_____

_____

Will I Buy It? Yes _____ No _____ Price $ _____

My Notes

Wine/Grape _____ (write in or circle below.)

White: Albariño, Chardonnay, Chenin Blanc, Gewürztraminer, Gruner Veltliner, Marsanne, Muscat, Palomino, Pinot Gris/Grigio, Prosecco, Riesling, Sauvignon Blanc/Fume Blanc, Semillon, Trebbiano, Verdicchio, Viognier

Red: Cabernet Franc, Cabernet Sauvignon, Gamay, Grenache, Malbec, Merlot, Mourvèdre, Nebbiolo, Petite Verdot, Pinot Noir, Pinotage, Sangiovese, Syrah/Petite Sirah/Shiraz, Tempranillo, Zinfandel

Color_____

Red, White, Blush, Rose

Appellation _____

The specific area in the world the grapes were grown. (e.g., Barossa Valley, Marlborough, Napa Valley, Rhone).

Name/Winery_____

The brand name is usually the winery name. They may be different or the same.

Vineyard/Estate _____

Vintage/Year _____

All grapes in the bottle must have been grown in this year.

My Comments _____

_____

_____

_____

Will I Buy It? Yes ____No ____ Price $ _____

My Notes

Wine/Grape _____ (write in or circle below.)

White: Albariño, Chardonnay, Chenin Blanc, Gewürztraminer, Gruner Veltliner, Marsanne, Muscat, Palomino, Pinot Gris/Grigio, Prosecco, Riesling, Sauvignon Blanc/Fume Blanc, Semillon, Trebbiano, Verdicchio, Viognier

Red: Cabernet Franc, Cabernet Sauvignon, Gamay, Grenache, Malbec, Merlot, Mourvèdre, Nebbiolo, Petite Verdot, Pinot Noir, Pinotage, Sangiovese, Syrah/Petite Sirah/Shiraz, Tempranillo, Zinfandel

Color_____

Red, White, Blush, Rose

Appellation _____

The specific area in the world the grapes were grown. (e.g., Barossa Valley, Marlborough, Napa Valley, Rhone).

Name/Winery_____

The brand name is usually the winery name. They may be different or the same.

Vineyard/Estate _____

Vintage/Year _____

All grapes in the bottle must have been grown in this year.

My Comments _____

_____

_____

_____

Will I Buy It? Yes ____No ____ Price $ _____

My Notes

Wine/Grape _____ (write in or circle below.)

White: Albariño, Chardonnay, Chenin Blanc, Gewürztraminer, Gruner Veltliner, Marsanne, Muscat, Palomino, Pinot Gris/Grigio, Prosecco, Riesling, Sauvignon Blanc/Fume Blanc, Semillon, Trebbiano, Verdicchio, Viognier

Red: Cabernet Franc, Cabernet Sauvignon, Gamay, Grenache, Malbec, Merlot, Mourvèdre, Nebbiolo, Petite Verdot, Pinot Noir, Pinotage, Sangiovese, Syrah/Petite Sirah/Shiraz, Tempranillo, Zinfandel

Color_____

Red, White, Blush, Rose

Appellation _____

The specific area in the world the grapes were grown. (e.g., Barossa Valley, Marlborough, Napa Valley, Rhone).

Name/Winery_____

The brand name is usually the winery name. They may be different or the same.

Vineyard/Estate _____

Vintage/Year _____

All grapes in the bottle must have been grown in this year.

My Comments _____

_____

_____

_____

Will I Buy It? Yes _____ No _____ Price $ _____

My Notes

Wine/Grape _____ (write in or circle below.)

White: Albariño, Chardonnay, Chenin Blanc, Gewürztraminer, Gruner Veltliner, Marsanne, Muscat, Palomino, Pinot Gris/Grigio, Prosecco, Riesling, Sauvignon Blanc/Fume Blanc, Semillon, Trebbiano, Verdicchio, Viognier

Red: Cabernet Franc, Cabernet Sauvignon, Gamay, Grenache, Malbec, Merlot, Mourvèdre, Nebbiolo, Petite Verdot, Pinot Noir, Pinotage, Sangiovese, Syrah/Petite Sirah/Shiraz, Tempranillo, Zinfandel

Color_____

Red, White, Blush, Rose

Appellation _____

The specific area in the world the grapes were grown. (e.g., Barossa Valley, Marlborough, Napa Valley, Rhone).

Name/Winery_____

The brand name is usually the winery name. They may be different or the same.

Vineyard/Estate _____

Vintage/Year _____

All grapes in the bottle must have been grown in this year.

My Comments _____

_____

_____

_____

Will I Buy It? Yes ____No ____Price $ _____

My Notes

Wine/Grape _____ (write in or circle below.)

White: Albariño, Chardonnay, Chenin Blanc, Gewürztraminer, Gruner Veltliner, Marsanne, Muscat, Palomino, Pinot Gris/Grigio, Prosecco, Riesling, Sauvignon Blanc/Fume Blanc, Semillon, Trebbiano, Verdicchio, Viognier

Red: Cabernet Franc, Cabernet Sauvignon, Gamay, Grenache, Malbec, Merlot, Mourvèdre, Nebbiolo, Petite Verdot, Pinot Noir, Pinotage, Sangiovese, Syrah/Petite Sirah/Shiraz, Tempranillo, Zinfandel

Color_____

Red, White, Blush, Rose

Appellation_____

The specific area in the world the grapes were grown. (e.g., Barossa Valley, Marlborough, Napa Valley, Rhone).

Name/Winery_____

The brand name is usually the winery name. They may be different or the same.

Vineyard/Estate _____

Vintage/Year _____

All grapes in the bottle must have been grown in this year.

My Comments_____

_____

_____

_____

Will I Buy It? Yes ____No ____ Price $ _____

My Notes

Wine/Grape _____ (write in or circle below.)

White: Albariño, Chardonnay, Chenin Blanc, Gewürztraminer, Gruner Veltliner, Marsanne, Muscat, Palomino, Pinot Gris/Grigio, Prosecco, Riesling, Sauvignon Blanc/Fume Blanc, Semillon, Trebbiano, Verdicchio, Viognier

Red: Cabernet Franc, Cabernet Sauvignon, Gamay, Grenache, Malbec, Merlot, Mourvèdre, Nebbiolo, Petite Verdot, Pinot Noir, Pinotage, Sangiovese, Syrah/Petite Sirah/Shiraz, Tempranillo, Zinfandel

Color_____

Red, White, Blush, Rose

Appellation _____

The specific area in the world the grapes were grown. (e.g., Barossa Valley, Marlborough, Napa Valley, Rhone).

Name/Winery_____

The brand name is usually the winery name. They may be different or the same.

Vineyard/Estate _____

Vintage/Year _____

All grapes in the bottle must have been grown in this year.

My Comments_____

_____

_____

_____

Will I Buy It? Yes ____No ____Price $ _____

My Notes

Wine/Grape _____ (write in or circle below.)

White: Albariño, Chardonnay, Chenin Blanc, Gewürztraminer, Gruner Veltliner, Marsanne, Muscat, Palomino, Pinot Gris/Grigio, Prosecco, Riesling, Sauvignon Blanc/Fume Blanc, Semillon, Trebbiano, Verdicchio, Viognier

Red: Cabernet Franc, Cabernet Sauvignon, Gamay, Grenache, Malbec, Merlot, Mourvèdre, Nebbiolo, Petite Verdot, Pinot Noir, Pinotage, Sangiovese, Syrah/Petite Sirah/Shiraz, Tempranillo, Zinfandel

Color_____

Red, White, Blush, Rose

Appellation _____

The specific area in the world the grapes were grown. (e.g., Barossa Valley, Marlborough, Napa Valley, Rhone).

Name/Winery_____

The brand name is usually the winery name. They may be different or the same.

Vineyard/Estate _____

Vintage/Year _____

All grapes in the bottle must have been grown in this year.

My Comments _____

_____

_____

_____

Will I Buy It? Yes _____No _____Price $ _____

My Notes

Wine/Grape _____ (write in or circle below.)

White: Albariño, Chardonnay, Chenin Blanc, Gewürztraminer, Gruner Veltliner, Marsanne, Muscat, Palomino, Pinot Gris/Grigio, Prosecco, Riesling, Sauvignon Blanc/Fume Blanc, Semillon, Trebbiano, Verdicchio, Viognier

Red: Cabernet Franc, Cabernet Sauvignon, Gamay, Grenache, Malbec, Merlot, Mourvèdre, Nebbiolo, Petite Verdot, Pinot Noir, Pinotage, Sangiovese, Syrah/Petite Sirah/Shiraz, Tempranillo, Zinfandel

Color_____

Red, White, Blush, Rose

Appellation _____

The specific area in the world the grapes were grown. (e.g., Barossa Valley, Marlborough, Napa Valley, Rhone).

Name/Winery_____

The brand name is usually the winery name. They may be different or the same.

Vineyard/Estate _____

Vintage/Year _____

All grapes in the bottle must have been grown in this year.

My Comments _____

_____

_____

_____

Will I Buy It? Yes _____No _____Price $ _____

My Notes

Wine/Grape _____ (write in or circle below.)

White: Albariño, Chardonnay, Chenin Blanc, Gewürztraminer, Gruner Veltliner, Marsanne, Muscat, Palomino, Pinot Gris/Grigio, Prosecco, Riesling, Sauvignon Blanc/Fume Blanc, Semillon, Trebbiano, Verdicchio, Viognier

Red: Cabernet Franc, Cabernet Sauvignon, Gamay, Grenache, Malbec, Merlot, Mourvèdre, Nebbiolo, Petite Verdot, Pinot Noir, Pinotage, Sangiovese, Syrah/Petite Sirah/Shiraz, Tempranillo, Zinfandel

Color_____

Red, White, Blush, Rose

Appellation _____

The specific area in the world the grapes were grown. (e.g., Barossa Valley, Marlborough, Napa Valley, Rhone).

Name/Winery_____

The brand name is usually the winery name. They may be different or the same.

Vineyard/Estate _____

Vintage/Year _____

All grapes in the bottle must have been grown in this year.

My Comments _____

_____

_____

_____

Will I Buy It? Yes _____ No _____ Price $ _____

Visit the Sassy Sommelier at
www.sassysommelier.com
or e-mail
sassysommelier@sassysommelier.com

Bibliography

Material was adapted from:

http://en.wikipedia.org/wiki/Wine_tasting

MacNeil, Karen. *The Wine Bible*; Workman Publishing, New York (2001).

http://www.international-wines.com/IFRAMEs/images/wtg.html

Simon, Joanna. *Wine an Introduction*, A Dorling Kindersley Book, New York (2001)

Senior Editor: Peter Lynch

Technical Editor: Bob Thompson